Especially for:

_____

From:

_____

A Simple Gift of Comfort

Healing Words for Difficult Times

Jane Kirkpatrick

Artwork by Michal Sparks

HARVEST HOUSE PUBLISHERS

EUGENE, OREGON

A Simple Gift of Comfort

Formerly *A Burden Shared*
Text Copyright © 2002 by Jane Kirkpatrick
Artwork Copyright © 2008 by Michal Sparks
Published by Harvest House Publishers
Eugene, Oregon 97402
www.harvesthousepublishers.com

ISBN-13: 978-0-7369-2232-6
ISBN-10: 0-7369-2232-6

Jane Kirkpatrick is a writer, speaker, teacher, and mental health professional. Please visit her website at www.jkbooks.com.

Design and Production by Garborg Design Works, Savage, Minnesota

Printed in China

08 09 10 11 12 13 14 15 / LP / 10 9 8 7 6 5 4 3 2 1

CONTENTS

WORDS OF COMFORT

The right word
spoken at the right
time is as beautiful
as gold apples
in a silver bowl.

I want to give you words of wisdom, offered to open your clear and perceptive mind.

I want to give you words of comfort, shared so you can feel the love so many have for you, to lift and buoy you in your swirling waters.

I want to give you words of joy, spoken to make your spirit laugh and see the brightness of a future filled with those who care.

I want to give you words of endurance, words to inspire you and support you through this time and yet to let you know I have great confidence in your courage and your competence.

I want to give you words to nourish your soul, place golden apples in your silver bowl.

*I*f I could find a way to be there, I would come; to listen while you told of what you'd done to help another, how your hands had touched and washed and tenderly directed. I would hold you while you spoke of powerlessness and pain, wipe your tears when you related that all you did could not hold on to what life gave you and then took away.

I'm not standing beside you now, not holding you in person. But I am with you. My arms embrace you. My prayers are sent to give you strength so you will know that you are loved and yes, admired, too, for all you did and do. And it's my deep hope that what I send to you will be enough to see you through.

*Y*ou are more to me than "friend," and yet I know no other word that says as much. You are a treasure in my chest of wealth. You honor energy, close connection and commitment, trust and hope. Your care stands firm; fired through the heat of change and distance, troubled times and tears. You are free of the veil of judgment. And if you could, I believe you'd hold me through the night as well and let me cry.

All that you would do for me, I would do for you. It is how we treat our priceless treasures. I would be a treasure to you.

*T*he view from our porch is pleasant, though we rarely took the time to notice until we sat to swing. Animals sleep. The river flows on. A tree grows without effort. Our souls are fed.

In these tornado times it can be difficult to find a place to sit and swing and let your soul be soothed. And yet it's needed: to notice what can happen without effort, that even in the midst of turmoil, tranquility flourishes.

If you do not have a porch swing in your life, a place to sit and rest and gather nourishment, please come sit on mine. Together we can find calm comfort.

I heard about it and felt the wash of sadness that must have cascaded over you when you learned; a sense of drowning, suffocating, and yet a pain so searing it could have been a thousand bee stings striking all at once.

If I could stand beside you now, I would; to deflect the waves of pain you don't deserve nor can you stop. I'd tell you that this pain will pass and hope that you'd believe me.

*Y*ou'll breathe again, remember when it did not hurt so much and inhale strength from memories as you take each breath. Until that moment comes when you begin to live again, I pray my heart, less broken, will beat soundly for both of us.

*I*t's in the little places where grief hides, jumps out to surprise us when we least expect. It's hidden in the scent of a sweater, a perfume, a food, the sound of the river at night. Grief huddles, then leaps into the flush of a flower, the melody of a song shared, the touch of a hand to a cheek. It explodes a memory thought put well away; it's the little things that bring back the pain.

My care for you in this troubling time is but a little thing in the scheme of what you face. Its packaging is small and may seem insignificant. But it is sturdy, strong, and never-ending. I bring it so you can hold it as assurance that the wounds will heal and you won't always hurt so deeply when grief surprises you from its hiding places in your world.

*W*omen sat and stitched. Their worn and wrinkled fingers pulled together pieces of her past cut into little squares: a child's worn dress, a bedroom curtain, a flowered tablecloth (with the berry stain her husband made one holiday cut out and now discarded). Dozens of memories they patched together.

They sewed the single-colored backing down. The comforter, completed, would keep her warm through winter's winds.

What comforts are the memories, the patches that mark the past and then are held together with the stitching hands of friends placed over solid backing. Surrounded by the fondness, we recall the memories, let them nourish us, keep us warm, and give us needed sleep; knowing in the morning we can set aside the quilt, rested, still wrapped in comfort.

In these difficult days, I give my comforter to you. May the memories you wish to savor wrap themselves around you, stitched together by the hands of friends.

*T*hey say that anger is an after-thought, one that follows loss. To calm the anger, to turn it into something purposeful and strong, the loss must first be counted and remembered, not trivialized or disclaimed. Only then can loss be grieved and allowed to change us.

Your loss is grievous. No words can fill the space you have nor ease the impact of the wound, and yet I'd spend the night with you to try to find the words to ease, the touch that heals. I suspect we would discover once again that life is not fair. Life only is.

You are special to me. The most that I can offer is to help you make the claim against your disappointment, lament its happening and the loss, and help you live again.

They shared a neighborhood and street, these friends; shared good memories, good times. When each wife became a widow within weeks of the other, they shared in mourning, too. Each agreed no hour would be too late to wake the other when the memories and loss became so great that only a friend's embrace could get them through. No need to call ahead, just knock on the other's door.

I would be that open to your needs, night or day, no need to call ahead, no need to arrange. And I know that you would be there to share my mourning too. In that way, our lives would meet, our shared healing would soothe life's wounds.

You who give so much to others, may you find
your own strength, faith, and flexibility
reflected in the lives of those you cherish.
You reach beyond yourself; you lend a helping hand.
You live your faith each day.
You are a warm and nourishing light
in what is sometimes a dark and dreary world.
I am grateful for the warmth the light
of your life has given me.

The word "abide" once
meant "to cover,"
to offer protection in
the way an eagle's wing
folds over its young.

I want to be a friend
that abides with you
today through prayer
and the process of
folding you into
my heart.

*W*ho's to say that interwoven, complex works of art contribute more or stay longer in the memory? Who's to say that shorter songs of rich and vibrant tones leave less behind when their melodies cease? Each is important in the music of our lives, no one greater than the other.

As you face this troubling time, I hope you listen to the music of what was, however long the symphony, however short the composition, and remember all the deep and enlightening notes. Let them linger and encourage you, a reminder that you will hear music again, sometime in the future.

THE BEST WE CAN HOPE FOR
IN OUR TIME OF NEED IS
TO ACCEPT HELP FROM OTHERS
AND THEN PASS LOVE ALONG.

SECTION
Two

NEW
BEGINNINGS

*There is a time
to mourn and
a time to dance.*

THE BOOK OF ECCLESIASTES

*F*irst the "why" arrives. Why me? Why this? Why now? Then comes the anger or regret, perhaps the bargain of how it will all go differently next time, if only this or that could happen now. Then comes the wrenching sadness like a fog that threatens to engulf. Finally, acceptance appears. Like the slow development of a photograph, the image becomes clearer until we recognize it for what it is.

Knowing, acknowledging, accepting, we can move on. We may step back a time or two, on an anniversary date, at the scent of something that brings this moment and this loss to mind. But the pain will lessen as it moves through time.

Such is the promise of a new beginning bound into the process of grief.

*T*he Acoma, indigenous people of North America, are known for their pottery of great beauty and strength. What distinguishes their pots from other pueblos' is the mix of the clay.

Grandmothers search the desert for shards of pottery once formed, fired, used, and then discarded. Lifting the broken pieces from beneath the sage and white sand, they grind the old shards into powder. The potters then mix the old powder with unfired new. The two clays—the old and the new together—are molded and when fired become the strongest pottery.

So we are formed, if we allow it. Old powder from our past experiences once thought useless, broken, lacking value, can be combined with new ones and through the fires of life, can give us strength.

I wish for you this kind of strength.

$\mathcal{I}$ can say "I love you," but it's how I act upon the words that tells you if what I say is true.

I wish that I could be there with you so you could see the way I feel. My arms would open to embrace you, my ears block out the sounds of this world so I could hear only what you wished to say. My fingertips will wipe the wetness from your cheeks. We will sigh together and take one deep breath and start again. It is a message of my care that I communicate in this difficult time.

A FRIEND HOLDS YOUR HANDS IN THEIR THOUGHTS AND THEIR PRAYERS.

An abundant wheat harvest would be remiss without plans for reseeding for the future. The best seed is always searched for in the harvest and then kept behind.

People need the privilege, too. A season promised for reseeding.

In this time that seems so far from harvest, I will help you find a seed worth saving. Together we'll plant the promise of tomorrow found inside the harvest of today.

*Y*ou may feel that you're inside a valley now, one suffocating and restricting. But I can see the possibilities in your vale, even if you never see the mountaintop. With ears tuned toward the future and no blowing sand to snarl the view, I would take a tour with you and help you seek mountaintop experiences in the lowlands of your life.

As you seek a place where pain and powerlessness are left behind, look for what is real and lasting. My care fits there, a fondness for you that bears no imitation but is meant to give refreshment in this difficult time.

The field's been plowed.

Now that you see it,

you wish that it had been left alone.

You imagine in your mind the way

the field looked green with virgin grass,

untilled.

But the field's been plowed,

and now it's time to plant anew.

Make it the best plowed field ever.

I'll work it with you.

Together we will produce a strong and worthy yield

by accepting all that is and moving on.

"What's done is done," says the octogenarian who lived through a financial collapse, a war, and the loss of a son. "Events cannot be brought back or changed. Only what this moment brings can I command and so I do it," the elder says.

Instead of giving up an hour to think of what could or should have been, the wise old soul makes a phone call to a friend. He fixes a bowl of soup and savors the aroma of the moment. He pays a bill and mails it; reads a book that brings on laughter; feeds the dog.

He fills the time with what he decides will give him strength, not what once was.

*Y*ou may think your time to flower has passed, that too many years or hard events will keep you from blooming more. But it is the lengthening of days that brings the bloom, not the endurance of the plant or even the vigilance of the gardener, though each contributes. It is additional light, added exposure to the nutrients of sun touching each plant's unique code that produces the flower, and later, the fruit.

When you see the yellows of chrysanthemums, or spring's lilac blues, please remember that you share this in common with the plants: blooms occur when living things are nourished by extended exposure to God's light. May today be the day you truly bloom.

*S*urviving, said women in a research study, meant living with loss, overcoming hard times, managing being different, and learning to put difficult things behind you. Their strength, they said, came not from enduring the hardships themselves, but from *how* they survived them. Especially important was the sustenance of close relationships, like going to a well for water.

They created a place where they could feel at home. They accomplished a valued task and allowed themselves to feel satisfaction. Being able to gather memories and reflect on life's patterns seemed to grant vitality.

You harbor that survivor spirit in your heart. You will survive this hard time.

GIFTS THAT ENCOURAGE

I watch you struggle,
seeking meaning and strong comfort.
Some of what you hope for seems to flee and fade away.
I ache for you then,
wanting the most for you.
I wish for you the deepest reach,
your arms opened,
your heart prepared for His strong love.
It is what I know will give you strength
and truly fill your soul.

$\mathcal{B}$abies are said to calm themselves to strains of Mozart or Chopin, even in the womb, and then select their favorites when those same songs are heard again in the nursery. At the other end of life, music brings old toes to tapping; feet and hands that might not have stirred for years pick up the beat. Music soothes and moves.

I hope you find the music in your life, that you will give yourself permission to take time to listen and be rested by the tones and tempos that best suit you. In troubling times, let the melodies make you more productive and take you back to memories of restful infancy; and forward, to anticipate the joyous dances of old age. Listen closely. I hear a song being played for you.

*I*t has the illusion of calm, the word "pastor" does, evoking images of peace and placid pastoral green dotted with the fleecy white of tranquil sheep.

But the word means "shepherd" in the German language. Its meaning draws strength from the caretaker, not the surrounding sheep or soil. The shepherd is a being who tends but also fights off predators. The shepherd aggressively seeks out wayward lambs. He reaches out to protect by preventing potentially poor choices.

Others might look upon your world today as placid and calm and cannot see the turmoil rolling inside you, the potential problems you are sorting through. I would urge you now to call upon the Shepherd in your life. He will pastor you through.

*F*amily. It has a dozen definitions, but it's taken from the Latin word *famulus* meaning "servant."

I may not be of your lineage, your bloodline; or one you'd call your kin, but I am willing to be family, your servant, in these difficult days. It would be my gift to counsel, listen, bring you nourishment, and help the throbbing in your head fade away by my presence, my good will for you, my wish to ease your days.

To you,

whose heart belongs to others,

who gives with joy and ease,

who seeks forgiveness without agitation

and trusts God for all provision:

you carry the homestead spirit

in your heart.

You have walked beside others with compassion and care. Your stride was broad enough to stimulate their efforts, though they were sometimes tired; yet small enough to stay abreast. You encouraged success.

I am willing to walk beside you now in your time of trial. I'll let you set the pace and encourage you to the end.

I'd prefer no fences between us, no rocks piled so high I cannot see the worry on your face, the way your shoulders bend with the weight of stones you carry, what tension hides within your hands.

But if you create a fence, I will respect it and not cross without invitation. But I hope you keep the barrier low. For then I can reach across, make my offer. If you accept it and balance me as I step over into your world of sadness or distress, I will bring my presence and my prayers. I will bring confidence, too, that while our fences stand between us, they need not separate us. I will do my best to keep the fences low so they never block the gifts friends bring, both helpfulness and hope.

*F*ields of corn are promises kept, the currency of care. Every silky, slippery thread that tops the stalk and lends itself to sun and rain leads directly beneath the shucks to the slender cob and an individual kernel. Without the wispy, almost unnoticeable silk, each tiny kernel could not exist, would not fulfill its promise. It could not be fertilized, its genetic code would not compute. On the cob, a bare spot would remain where a plump and moisture-laden kernel was meant to be.

I think the corncob says we can have assurance that the God who designed the cornstalk down to the tiny details has the power and will to care that much for us. Every kindness, every helping hand, every moment when another reaches out to touch our spirit with nourishment and warmth are simply silky threads meant to bring inspiration deep inside the souls we clothe beneath our skins.

*I*f I fix it, I take away your chance to use the tools you think fit best to repair it as you'd like. If I fix it, I deprive you of the knowledge you can think and act creatively, find inspiration in the depths of disappointment. You might well resent my meddling in this building project called "your life."

I won't be a fixer because I can't and I shouldn't. Neither will I let my eyes belie a patronizing attitude about your lack of builder skills. But I will loan you tools and wisdom of my experience and be your finest "go-for" ever, to offer what you need to remodel this hard time into a living space of open, soaring ceilings held firm by strong, protective walls.

My German grandmother

translated the word "depression"

as "strong courage."

May you discover strength

in this time of depression,

and may the wisdom of your years

unveil your valor, too.

MOMENTUM

*"Focus" comes from an old
word meaning hearth,
the center of the home.
The farther from the hearth one
moves, the colder one gets.
Remember where the fire is.
It will keep you focused
in this troubled time.*

You don't have to climb the mountain today, only find the footholds that will greet you in the morning. You don't have to graduate today, only take that first class. You don't have to write a novel, just pen a paragraph. Somehow we seem to think we must be large enough to finish before we first begin.

We gain by just beginning, take on new strength with each small step taken, even if we have to later change our course. Clarity and direction rise from the swirl of indecision; courage and potency appear through the malaise of unworthiness and woe.

Your faith need not be strong enough to finish, only adequate to embark.

We can take the next first step together.

*G*iven as a gift, the blue tarp once provided shade. Later, it covered irrigation pumps put up for the winter. When it began to shred, it offered filtered light, a flash of color over the dog run. The wind whipped it further, and it should have been discarded as the blue strings drifted in the breeze. It was useless, but we didn't toss it away.

In the fall, when the wind blew leaves off a nearby tree, we discovered new meaning from the tarp. Hanging in the tree that towered over the kennel were blue nests. The birds had taken what we'd thought useless and formed new baskets of color in the poplar tree.

That's what love is, I think: to take what might have seemed unworthy, past its prime, and turn it into nurture. When all the leaves are gone and you feel stripped and bare, I'll be there wearing blue, offering my love to you.

Even strong, deep-rooted trees
must bend in the wind
or be torn from the soil.
Your world is buffeted by gale forces.
Please don't think that strength
cannot hold gentleness and rest.
It can.
Lean into me.
Together we can weather this.

In times of trouble, you often step out to walk beside others with kindness and care. May you know today that someone wishes to walk beside you. You give a gift when you let them.

*S*tudents learning the art of basket-making have a tradition: they give their first completed basket away, often to their master basket teacher.

What kind of person inspires such gifts? Someone who would not judge my work harshly. Someone comfortable finding good woven with bad, who sees promise and potential hidden inside effort. A person who will tell me what I've made is worthy just because it comes from me.

It is the greatest gift of love to relinquish the first fruits of our creation; the greatest gift of trust to offer someone a portion of ourselves that's less than perfect. It's an act of courage and devotion. It's what we do when we admit our faults and ask forgiveness. It's what happens when another accepts us as we are.

Daily, we make first baskets woven of our experiences, our hopes and disappointments. Daily, we have a Teacher willing to accept our efforts.

*B*rody, the Labrador, jumps and barks with the sound of food pellets rolling into his bowl. His excitement would make a stranger think he'd never been fed, a fact his ninety-six pounds belies. Later, lifting the leash turns him inside out, he anticipates his walk. The sight of a mud puddle lures him to splashing ecstasy. The dog's joy honors everyday events. He isn't troubled by repetition and routine. He craves it.

In difficult times, the dog is a reminder that joy explodes from the familiar, not as tedium, but as triumph. It is hidden in the simple and routine. May you recognize it as the sun warms your face or raindrops wash against your cheeks. May it enter your senses in the sweet smell of an infant after her bath, in the sweep of leaves from the driveway, cool tile against your bare feet. May you find in your daily tasks today, not the drudgery of obligation, but the exuberance of a Labrador. The common in a time of turmoil, can bring the greatest peace.

$\mathcal{T}$he carpenter's coping saw is formed of steel forged as thin as a child's ribbon. Used to fit things into tight places, like cabinets into corners, the blade must be both strong and flexible. Too strong, and it will splinter what needs to be fit; too flexible and unwanted gaps will remain. To cope successfully, the blade must demonstrate this strength and flexibility. It is the balanced combination of these two characteristics that allows the saw to change direction quickly and without friction.

The coping saw speaks to life as well....We need to know when to stand firm and when to bend a bit, change direction, back off to let God make the fit.

WEEPING MAY ENDURE
FOR A NIGHT, BUT JOY
COMES IN THE MORNING.

PSALM 30:5 NKJV

*T*here are mosaics in a marriage, patterns that define uniqueness and reflect the seasons of a couple's years. The places they fished or golfed, the stories told of first meetings and falling in love, hard times, and change. Such marriage stories preserve tradition and transport a family's cultural value and beliefs from one generation to the next. Patterns. They tell stories and offer meaning.

Misfortune, hardship, grief, and trouble have their patterns, too. From them we learn to seek the message inlaid within the worry and the work that comes with living. Wisdom appears, emerges from the lessons scratched across the slates of our lives.

Strength lives inside mosaics, too; within the patterns layered upon life. I would be a part of your mosaic, help you find the pattern that will tell you what should happen next, what step to take, how to proceed. It is your pattern, your story.

You are the author of the next chapter.

DREAMS AND RISKS

*May neither the
errors of your past
nor the terrors of
your future keep
you from walking where
God's spirit leads you.*

*Y*ou risked, stretched yourself, and some might say, you'd failed. But if all we chanced promised perfection, there'd be no need for human beings, we'd just use machines to decide the direction we should take.

You proved your humanness and hopefulness, and I admire your choice to risk no matter how others rate results. You inhaled life and exhaled inspiration.

*"For I know
the plans I have for you,"
declares the Lord,
"plans to prosper you and not to harm you,
plans to give you hope and a future."*

JEREMIAH 29:11 NIV

The capacity to dream and take the dream from wispiness to real lives inside hardy spirits. A commitment makes it easier to withstand the storms that blast our sailing ships or the fires that consume the things we've cared for in the dark of night. A firm decision pulls us like a beacon toward it, so disasters only change the path we take, not the destination.

You have made a worthy commitment. Now when the dream seems distant, when turmoil threatens, let commitment be the light you follow through the gloom. Do not mistake this darkness for the final destination.

*K*nowing what we control and what we don't will make us hardy. When disappointment swipes, when abandonment and loss come riding by, when the river rises out of season or drought steals all the harvest, hardy people become powerful. Hardy people recognize a challenge as a teacher bringing needed instruction, even guidance, and the chance to deepen wisdom or expand inventiveness. They ask what action they can take, how to respond; not "why me?" "why this?" "why now?" They spend little time assigning blame. Lament and blame only keep hardy people from their commitments.

I know it seems much is now beyond what you control. Still, I hope you see your choices, however small and insignificant they might appear. I hope you choose to become a hardy spirit.

Kelpies are stock dogs. Short, close to the ground, a kelpie can still jump six feet into the air. Loyal, duty-bound, they're used for herding sheep and cattle. Because they're light and yet can leap, they clear the fences between pens and run across the backs of sheep to where they need to be to keep the peace, leaving behind no evidence they stepped on fleecy backs.

With cows, the little dogs nip at the nose or heels of animals one hundred times their body weight or size. They are fearless, taking on predators known for fierceness but not backing off, snapping at air with their powerful jaws. Yet at day's end, they lie about with children without bother. The kelpie knows its duty and direction and trusts it has been given all it needs to do its job.

I wish for you today the confidence of the kelpie; the clear commitment to your task, the courage to face foes twice your size, and to soar over barriers with grace.

MAY YOU FIND TODAY'S CHALLENGE THE OPPORTUNITY YOU'VE BEEN SEEKING, NOT THE TRAGEDY THAT YOU FEARED.

*B*ones of the greater Canada goose are porous and light, designed to hold the air they breathe inside and keep them airborne. They fly farther and remain in the air longer because of these feather-light bones. The bird's engineering and design, its capacity to take in air and flush it through its body is a marvel and an inspiration.

"Inspiration" means the act of breathing in.

Be inspired today. Take a deep breath and let it fill your lungs, course through your arteries to feed your body and your brain. No shallow gasps, but a deep intake of breath, an inspiration.

You will fly higher and go farther than you ever thought you could for we, too, are engineered in marvelous ways.

❋ ❋ ❋

*T*he warning of a flood means look for higher ground.

Today, I'm standing where it's safe and dry. I'm not affected as you are by the rising waters. I can see them, but they do not threaten here above the banks. Look for me. I'm reaching out to you. I'm standing where the ground is stable. I can see beyond the rushing waters to where the world looks familiar, recognizable, and more predictable. Some

ground has been washed away; new soil deposited to rebuild a once
fragile field.

I have saved a place for you, knowing when I face my flood, you
will do the same for me.

Higher, solid ground is what a friend can offer in a flood. Advance
a new perspective. I give that now to you. This too will pass, but I
will still be here to stand beside you as we rebuild together.

I know you feel disconnected today, full of dread and wonder; and you may think your goal is to eliminate all stress, to be detached from all turmoil. But disconnection never raised a responsible child, never cured a rare disease, never built a business or a nation. Perhaps surrender is the goal: surrender to what we can't control and surrender to the little twinge of nervousness that makes us act for change. You can make a difference, not despite your anxious moments, but because of them. I can hardly wait to see how creatively anxiety will act out in you today!

Artists often say they feel exposed when they perform, read their works, or hang their paintings in a gallery. But musicians, poets, writers, painters all agree, the risk's a worthy one. The exposure of our deepest selves can be the gift that touches others, brings a healing moment, directs someone to a place of strength or comfort, even necessary action.

Grief seems like that too, for some: a painful unmasking of our inner being that leaves us vulnerable and uncovered, fearful others will judge us and then pull away. And yet by sharing it, we have the chance to heal ourselves and reach another wounded soul.

When you come upon that dark place in the night that invites exposure of your grief, please know this: I will stay with you until the morning light, to reassure you that, even with unmasking, you are cared for just the way you are, though vulnerable and exposed.

JOURNEY INTO HOPE

*Carry each
other's burdens,
and in this way
you will fulfill
the law of Christ.*

*T*he mariposa lily spears the desert sand in June and stands, a purple throat, straight and exposed. It bends but never breaks despite the pressures of hot, sandy winds. Notably, the lily does not bloom each year, responding to some God-given code for its flowering time. But it blooms most often and is the most vibrant following winters distressed with cold and suffocating snows.

As I think of you, I consider the lily and know this, too, will pass.

*Y*ou are on a journey, thrust forward with old baggage from the past, filled with things not even needed where you're headed. Journeys are like that, asking us to pack familiar baggage even though it wears us down.

We may tell ourselves we want off at the nearest stop. Everything challenges our confidence and even our faith. But destinations are reached, even new and unexpected ones.

In whatever part of the journey you're on, know that others have walked before you. They've survived, with assurance and surprise.

*C*hange.

Like the slow rising of the river
after an early snowmelt in the
mountains, it seeps into our lives,
unhurried, almost without notice,
until the strength and breadth of it
covers everything that had once been
familiar, makes it different, new over
old. No rushing torrents, just slow-
rising water, licking at foundations.

What floods and change share
in common is the aftermath, the
need to rearrange the way things
used to be.

In this time of transformation,
I would help you rearrange and give
you assurance that one thing remains
unaltered: my care for you, whether
you're in the midst of a flash flood or
a slow-rising river.

So what do you pack for life's journey? Enough memories of friends and family to warm you in unfamiliar places. Enough time to notice the newness and not be frightened by its unfamiliarity. Enough patience to remember others are traveling, too, and that there's no prize for being first. Pack alternatives. There may be detours. You may not reach your destination on time. And pack a notebook so you can record the highlights of this road you're on, inspiring others to step out into the unknown. Please remember to save room for all the lessons learned that you'll be bringing back, lessons to help me pack for my journeys, too.

Family may fail us; occupation fall short; even our drive for sufficiency, fame, and good fortune will tumble down. Only inside, where the soul opens wide to the Spirit of God, will we discover our true place of belonging.

You do not have to travel alone. Let Him help you on your soul-filling journey toward belonging.

I would take it from you, if I could,
tie it up and throw it overboard. Together,
we could watch it sink. I might toss a life
raft to you, hoping I could help someone
I value.

Or would it just be a way of relieving
my pain that comes from watching you learn
how to handle discord? What message do I
send when I throw out a life raft when you
are simply learning how to swim? Does it
suggest that you might drown without me?
Or do I just deprive you of your own
discovery that you know how to stay afloat?

Maybe what you need is not a rescuer,
but someone cheering while you learn how
to breaststroke toward the shore? Hear
me? I'm that little voice far in the distance
encouraging and rejoicing, and I will be
holding the towel as you step triumphant on
the beach.

*W*here mighty rivers meet the ocean tides, the surf is powerful and rough, the place of transition marked with a bar invisible to the untrained eye. Even giant ships with experienced crews and wise old pilots have been known to flounder and succumb to the thunderous crash of waves there.

You are in that place where forces meet, change and disappointment clashing against a wish to keep things in familiar ways and places. It is a power struggle not unlike the ocean tides pounding against rivers.

I will be there if you let me. If you ask, I will help you set the course, act as crew or wear the pilot's badge as someone who has crossed through troubled waters and survived. And I will hold you in my thoughts, even after the waters calm.

*G*ardeners know the time to stake a plant is when it's small and slender, standing straight without a hint that it would ever later bend or break. That's when support is planned for, in the early days of tender, rapid growth that anticipates the winds it doesn't yet feel.

I would be a stake beside you, to bolster you against the gales, a reminder that you are in a growing place that brings turbulence and whirlwinds with it. I would be a stake that says you do not stand alone.

*W*hen someone is going through difficult times, the words of anthropologist Margaret Mead are cast with new meaning. She wrote that the earliest signs of civilization are not the tools or bowls uncovered from the dust of time, but the discovery of healed bones found within the caves or graves of old ones. That a bone could break and heal meant someone had to care enough to carry water, bring in food, fend off enemies, encourage, and daily move the injured from their pallets when the morning pain forced them to call out the name of one who cared. I will be there when you call out the name of one who cares.

*I*t's said that an early meaning of the prefix "com" as in "communion" was "to share burdens." The very word "communion" means to share and exchange, to give and take. It seems that's what we do when we listen to another, truly hear them with our hearts. And when we share the pain and strain of days, we find our load is lighter. We have communed.

In Latin, *com panis* means "with bread," two words so much a part of being a companion, the sharing of food, life-giving food. "Companion" carries with it meaning such as helpmate and ally, acquaintance and friend. If the prefix rings true, "companion" must mean a willingness to share the burdens, too.

I am willing to share your burdens. For if you let me be your companion during these difficult days, we will commune and share a togetherness meant to lift with compatible compassion.

*S*haped like a whirlwind and woven with twists of willows, tules, and tradition, the burden basket once fit on a Native Indian woman's back. A leather strap across her forehead held the basket steady. She carried only essentials inside, what was needed for huckleberry picking or gathering greasewood or seeds. Few things fit in the narrow bottom; most essentials were visible near the top. Those who walked beside her could see if her shoulders bent with the bulk of her burdens or could tell, even without words, if her head ached from the weight. Assistance could be offered. And so two could walk together toward their destination, helping to bear each other's burdens.

Please place your troubles near the surface so another can offer to share your load. "It's such an old burden," you say. "So heavy. I'm used to carrying it this way." And so you walk stooped over, too tired to set your basket down for just a moment while you run and play. Old habits cling to old burdens. To share them, we must be willing to shift our load.

I see your worries now are deep and that you feel strong enough to carry on alone. I will not rob you of your accomplishment. But I will walk beside you, watch for signs you ache. I'll periodically suggest a shift, select a shady spot to rest. I am here. I am willing. And if you should share your burden, I will be forever honored by this deepest sign of trust.

$\mathcal{A}$nd when I pray for you and with you, listen to your worries, and then go my separate way, I know you will not be left alone. A Comforter is promised, one to hold you ever after. My prayers are answered by a Counselor's presence even when friends and family are out of sight. You can speak and share at will. You are promised a power far greater than any my meager strength could leave.

My prayers for you are answered by love, unconditional and all sufficient. I leave no greater gift than my willingness to hold you in my prayers. You are there now and will be through this hard time.

NOTES